This book belongs to:
_____

This book is dedicated to all students. We hope you love your teachers as much as we know they love you.

This book is also dedicated to my friend Maddox. Thank you for inspiring me to write this second book. Your love for your teachers and your school is infectious!

-T.G.

For Mrs. Kotzen

-K.G.

© 2023 Tori Gelbert Publishing
Culpeper, Virginia
Text copyright © 2023 by Tori Gelbert Illustration copyright ©2023 by Katie Gigliotti
All rights reserved. No part of this publication may be reproduced, distributed, or transmitted in any form or by any means, including photocopying, recording, or other electronic or mechanical methods, without prior written permission of the author, except in the case of brief quotations embodied in critical reviews and certain other noncommerical uses permitted by copyright law.

ISBN: 979-8-9886586-1-0
LCCN: 2023912839
Library of Congress Cataloging-in-Publication Data on file.

For permission requests, contact Tori Gelbert at tori.gelbert@gmail.com

They think about you
in the morning,

at lunch,

and at their bedtime too.

They think about how to teach everyone,

At times you'll need help
when you're feeling blue;

and believe in you.

They'll always be there to help you learn,

and they'll remind you every grade is earned.

Don't worry when things get tough,

And whenever you're having a bad day

they'll continue to be there
and know what to say.

They'll help you learn math

and to become a great reader

so always remember...

be nice to your teacher!

...and this idea isn't new, but be nice to your principal too!

Tori Gelbert is a principal of an elementary school in Culpeper, VA. Her first book, "The Giraffe Who Loved School," was a book that encouraged children to create goals for themselves and to work hard to accomplish their goals, even when it may be difficult. For this book, she wanted to highlight the love and encouragement she knows all teachers, especially the amazing teachers at her school, give students daily.

A child at heart, Katie Gigliotti has taken her love for doodling to the next level by writing and illustrating several picture books including; Wander World, & You are. Also an art teacher, she knows just how selfless and wonderful teachers are. She would like her students, past and present, to know she thinks about them often and hopes they never give up on their dreams. You can find out more at katiegigliotti.com

WAYS TO SHOW YOUR TEACHER APPRECIATION

- 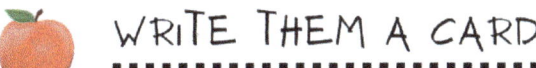 WRITE THEM A CARD
- 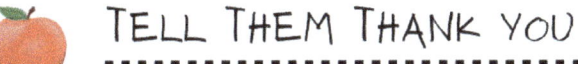 TELL THEM THANK YOU
- 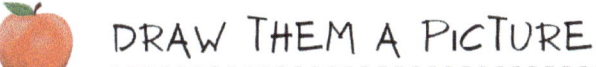 DRAW THEM A PICTURE
- 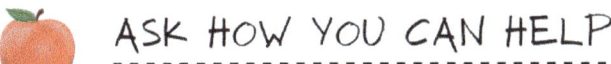 ASK HOW YOU CAN HELP
-  PICK A FLOWER FOR THEM

ALL ABOUT MY TEACHER

This is my teacher

My teacher is good at:

My teacher's name is:

What I love about my teacher:

A fun fact about my teacher:

My teacher likes:

THERE IS AN APPLE ON EACH PAGE OF THIS BOOK.
GO BACK AND SEE IF YOU CAN FIND THEM ALL!

www.ingramcontent.com/pod-product-compliance
Lightning Source LLC
Chambersburg PA
CBHW061406010526
44119CB00011B/269